300 PROGRESSIVE SIGHT READING EXERCISES FOR TRUMPET
Volume 1

The primary goal of this book is to train the ability to read music and to free the musician from being dependent on tablatures or other communication systems that are not used in the academic or professional worlds. This book has been designed to train aural skills concurrently with reading skills.

Preview, instructions, video lessons and more:

www.RobertAnthonyPublishing.com

Instructional video links will be posted on this site as videos are produced.

If this book is helping you, please post a positive review at whichever website you had purchased it from. If you have requests, suggestions, or constructive criticism, feel free to use the email link on my website to let me know.

Free pdf downloads of manuscript, tab paper, keyboard and fretboard diagrams, and so on are available on my website.

www.RobertAnthonyPublishing.com

Table of Contents

Foreword:

Volume One is comprised of 300 progressive eight-bar exercises that cover the keys signatures of C, G, F, D, Bb, A, and Eb Major and their relative minor keys and modes. Time signatures include 4/4 (Common Time), 3/4, 2/4, 6/8, and 2/2 (Cut Time).

While this book is intended to train sight-reading skills, it may also be used by beginners or those new to reading to acquire basic reading skills. It starts at a very basic level and adds a new note, rhythm, or concept every couple of pages and thoroughly reinforces them throughout the rest of the book.

The exercises are all eight measures (two phrases, or one period) in length. While they are composed to be melodic and pleasant to the ear, they are also composed to be difficult to memorize, and utilize many rhythms that seem to be absent from other sight reading books.

Instructions and a free preview are available in pdf form at:

www.RobertAnthonyPublishing.com

Finally, there are many correct ways to use this book. The instructions and a preview in pdf form are posted on my website so that I can update the instructions as I discover additional strategies. For example, I sometimes receive emails in which people tell me how they like to use this book. My opinions will evolve the more I use this book to train my students, so I want the ability to easily update the instructions as needed. The link for the pdf download will be directly below the picture of the cover of this book. Instructional videos supporting this book will be posted, as they are created, in the same place.

Major Scales

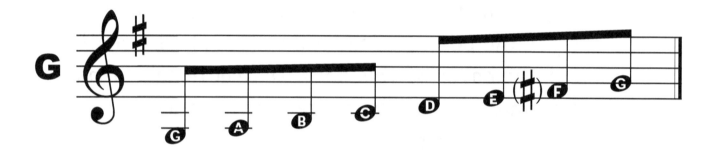

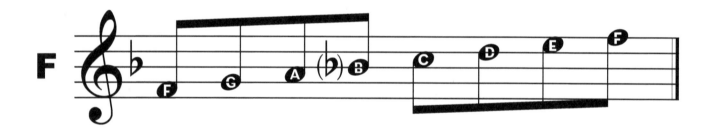

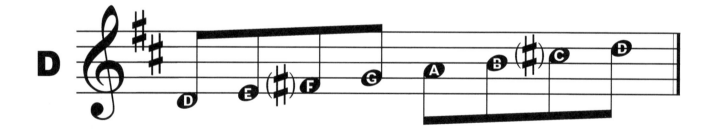

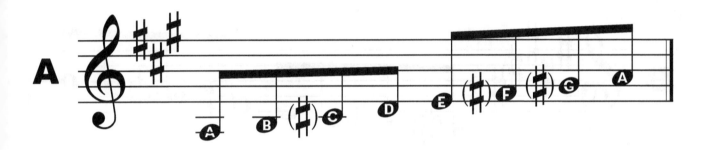

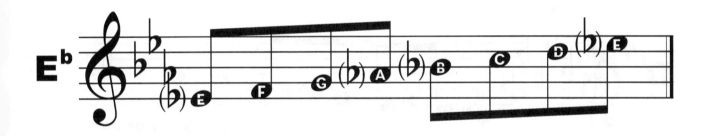

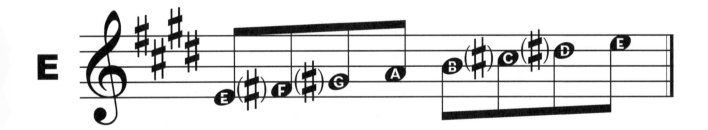

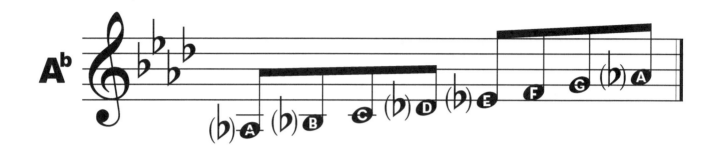

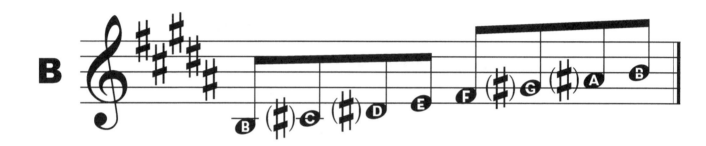

Circle of Fifths

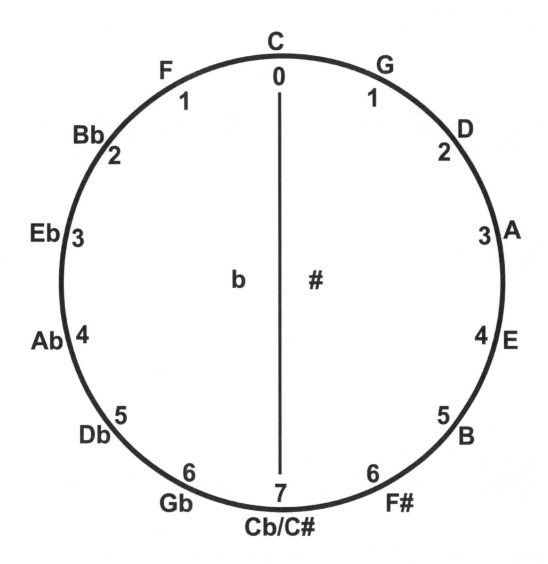

You can use the Circle of Fifths to recognize key signatures by how many sharps (#) or flats (b) are in the key. The key of A Major has three sharps, for example, and the key of Bb has two flats. In the key signatures, sharps always occur in the order: F C G D A E B, while flats always occur in the opposite order: B E A D G C F. Level One uses only the keys of C (no sharps or flats) and G (All Fs are sharped). Sharps make a note one key higher, while flats make a note one key lower.

The following sentence will help you to memorize these orders:

Frank's Cat Got Drunk At Elmo's Bar

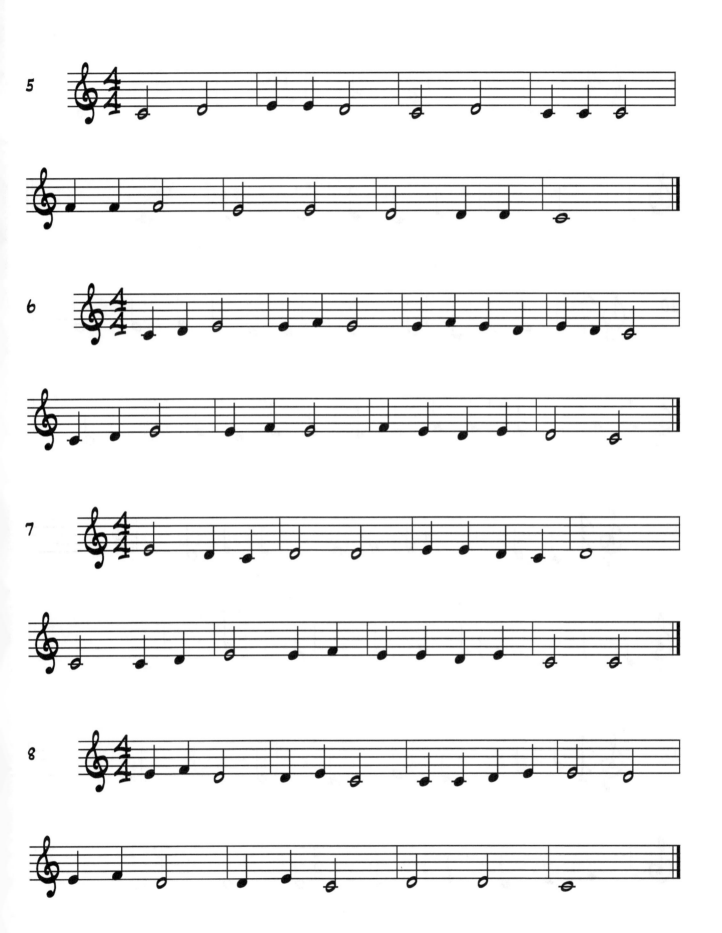

11

14

16

57

58

59

60

25

65

66

67

68

26

93

94

95

96

33

37

46

50

52

57

58

213

214

215

216

63

221

222

223

224

65

233

234

235

236

71

253

mp

mf

254

p

mf

255

mp

f

256

mf

p

73

82

83

84

Glossary of Musical Terms

Adagio: slowly
Allegretto: fairly fast
Allegro: fast
Andante: moderately slow
Andantino: usually faster than andante
Animato: lively, animated
Cantabile: in a singing style
D.C. al Fine: repeat from the beginning until fine
Dolce: sweetly
Expressivo: expressively
Fine: the end
Grave: very slow, solemnly
Grazioso: gracefully
Lento: very slow
Mesto: sad
Moderato: Medium Tempo
Ritard: slow down
Très Expressif: very expressive
Vivace: lively
Waltz: in three

Dynamic Markings

Pianissimo ~ pp: very softy
Piano ~ p: softly
Mezzo Piano ~ mp: moderately soft
Mezzo Forte ~ mf: moderately loud
Forte ~ f: loud
Fortissimo ~ ff: very loud

Identifying Note Names in Treble Clef

Traditional Approach

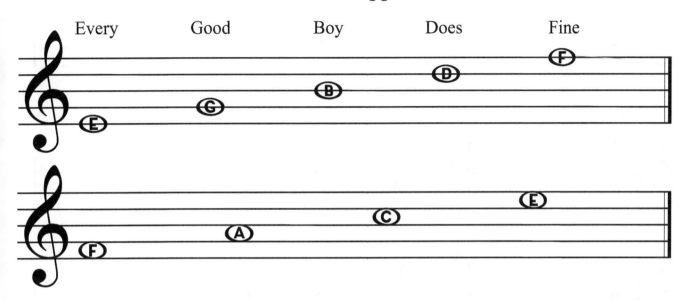

While the traditional approach above is helpful, you will likely find it to be easier to be aware that the musical alphabet (ABCDEFG) simply ascends the lines and spaces of the staff.

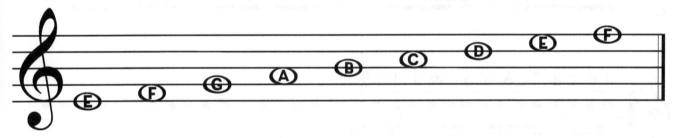

Ledger lines are used to extend the range of the staff as pictured here:

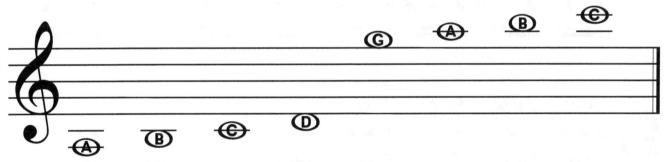

Counting Rhythms in 4/4

Counting Rhythms in 3/4

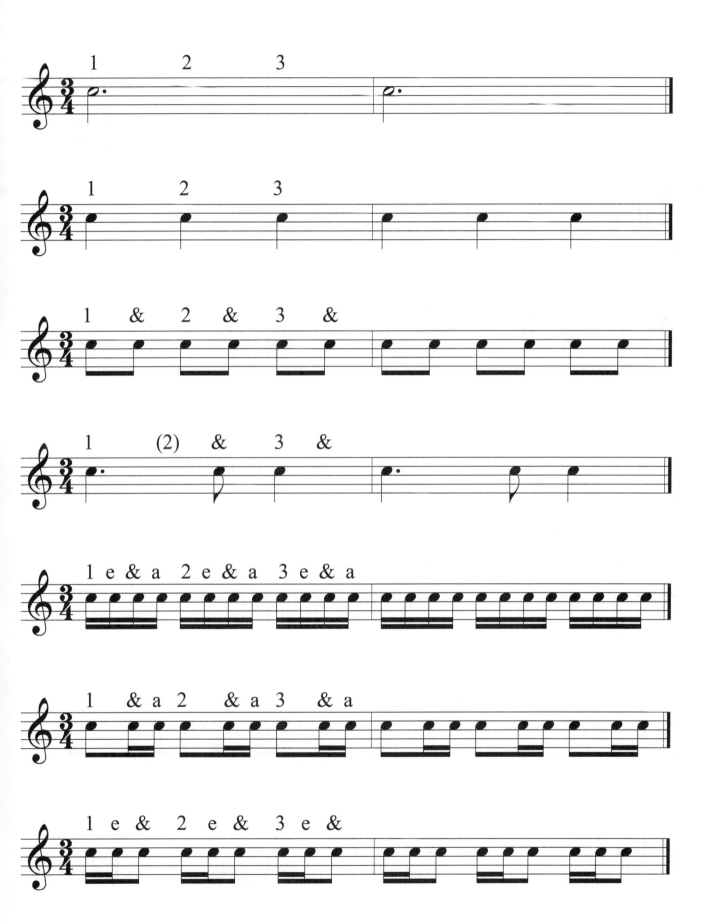

89

Counting Rhythms in 6/8

Counting Rhythms in 3/8

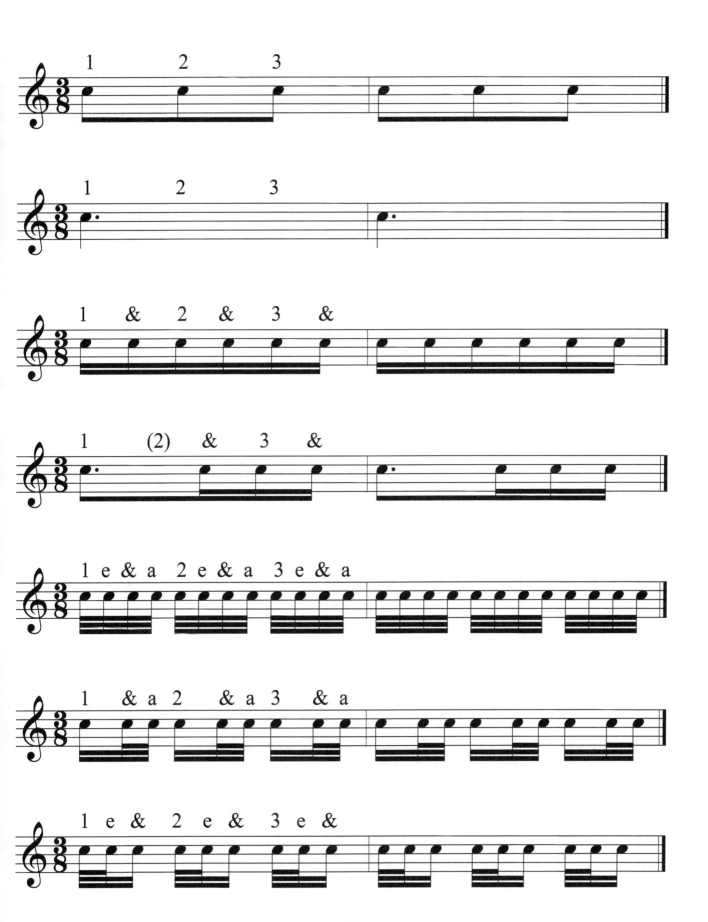

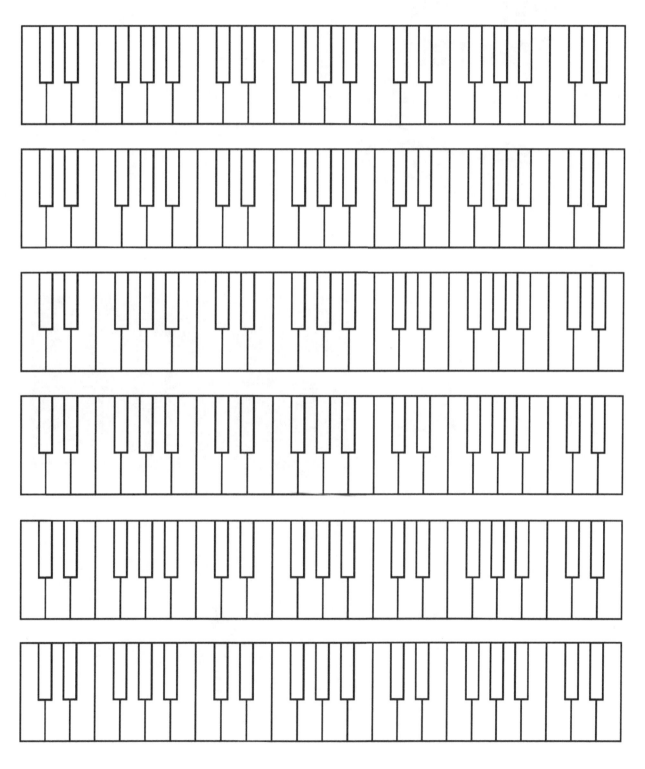

For those who need the easiest possible place to begin acquiring the ability to read music.

All signatures up to six sharps and six flats, with each key signature starting at the same beginning level.

27158626R00053